I Love This Tree

Franklin Watts
Published in Great Britain in 2016 by
The Watts Publishing Group

Copyright © The Watts Publishing Group, 2015

Credits
Editor: Sarah Peutrill
Designers: Chris Fraser and Cathryn Gilbert
Cover designer: Peter Scoulding
Picture researcher: Diana Morris
Illustrations: Andy Elkerton

Dewey number: 582.1'6
ISBN 978 1 4451 5265 3

Franklin Watts
An imprint of
Hachette Children's Group
Part of The Watts Publishing Group
Carmelite House
50 Victoria Embankment
London EC4Y 0DZ

An Hachette UK Company
www.hachette.co.uk
www.franklinwatts.co.uk

Printed in China

MIX
Paper from
responsible sources
FSC® C104740

Picture credits: Alberthep/istockphoto: 54c. Alinari/Topfoto: 50t. Alisbalb/Dreamstime: 28bl. Alphonsusjimos/Dreamstime: 47bc. Janez Ambrozic/Dreamstime: 28cl. Ansis/Dreamstime: 27t. Antarsis/Dreamstime: 36b. Arco Images/Alamy: 31t. Noam Arman/Dreamstime: 56bl. Arnau2098/Dreamstime: 29bra. Arterra PL/Alamy: 31br. Atelopus/istockphoto: 8b, 9b. Ken Backer/Dreamstime: 29rc. Marlyn Barbout/ Shutterstock: 14cbc. Aleksey Baskakov/Dreamstime: 32c. Scott Bauer/USDA Agricultural Research Service/Bugwood.org: 55. Benjitheijneb/ Wikimedia: 14cl. billberryphotography/istockphoto: 43tr. www.biolib.de/wikimedia: 32b, 33t, 33b. botii/istockphoto: 28tr. Mel Bradstock/ Shutterstock: 42cr. Simon Bratt/Shutterstock: 24cl. Ernest Brooks/IWM: 13b. Yuriy Brykaylo/Alamy: 32t. Dr Jeremy Burgess/SPL: 34b, 41b. Maximillian Busan/Dreamstime: 54br. Buyandlarge/SuperStock: 59c. Byrdyak/istockphoto: 25t. Kenneth William Caleno/Shutterstock: 56br. Chiuacat/Dreamstime: 4. Whitney Cranshaw/Colorado State University/Bugwood.org: 54cl. chungking/Shutterstock: 40bcl. Bill Davenport/ Dreamstime: 51t. dentdelion/istockphoto: 41t. Design 56/istockphoto: 14crb. Doleo8/istockphoto: 28tl. driftlessstudio/istockphoto: 29bl. Redmond Durrell/Alamy: 38-39t. E & E Images/HIP/Topfoto: 59t. Ulf Eliasson/CC Wikimedia Commons. Some rights reserved.: 42bl. Eng101/Dreamstime: 46tr. Andrey Eremin /Shutterstock: 47r. Carl Saltzmann Erste/CC. Wikimedia Commons: 12br. F Espenak/NASA/ GSFC: 8c. Howard Ensign Evans/Colorado State University/Bugwood.org: 39c. clémentfaugier.fr: 12cl. LaureniFochetto/istockphoto: 24bl. fotokon/istockphoto: 22b. Fotomak/Shutterstock: 14cba. John Fowler: 30b. Erik Gauger/istockphoto: 17tc. GlobaP/istockphoto: front cover tl, 40tl. gniedzieska/istockphoto: 40bl. Cao Hai/Dreamstime: 23c. Linda Haugen/USDA Forest Service/Bugwood.org: 53t. www.blog. nathanhaze.com: 14crb. HorderRehab: 25b. Patricia Hunter/Dreamstime: 43b. Ikiwaner/CC Wikimedia Commons. Some rights reserved: 29cr. imagedb.com/Shutterstock: 37t. Imagewise/Rex Features: 49tr. Brocken Inaglory/CC Wikimedia Commons. Some rights reserved: 31cr. Bill Ingalls/NASA: 14bl. IWM: 13c. Holger Karius/Dreamstime:48c. Steven Katovich/USDA Forest Service/Bugwood.org: 38bl. KatPaws/ istockphoto: 17c. Kenpei /CC Wikimedia Commons. Some rights reserved: 42cl. Ilya Ktsn/Flickr/CC. Wikipedia: 9cl. Andrey Kunca/ National Forest Centre Slovakia/Bugwood.org: 53b. Paul Lampard/Dreamstime: 50b. Edith Layland/Dreamstime: 28tlb. Lizst Collection/ Topfoto: 13t. Becca MacDonald/Sault College/Bugwood.org: 40obcl. Paul Maguire/Dreamstime: 28clb. Maite Lohmann/Dreamstime: 24c. Cosmin Manci/Shutterstock: front cover br. Thomas Marent/Minden Pictures/FLPA: 39b. Andrija Markovic/Dreamstime: 20t. Yon Marsh/ Alamy: 23t. Mikhail Melnikov/Shutterstock: front cover bl, back cover tl, cr & br. Mhfoto/Dreamstime: 29trb. Mikelane45/Dreamstime: 54bl. Mohylek/CC Wikimedia Commons. Some rights reserved: 29tc. Mike Murphy/CC. Wikipedia Commons. Some rights reserved: 10r. Museum of Toulouse/CC. Wikimedia Commons:, Some rights reserved. 18t, 45c. nadlyaizat/istockphoto: 37b. NASA: 13cr. B Navrez/ CC Wikimedia Commons. Some rights reserved: 42t. Noluma/istockphoto: 50c. Safak Oguz/istockphoto: 14cr. James Osmond/Alamy: 24t. paisan191/istockphoto: 16t. panbazil/Shutterstock: back cover bl. Jerry A Payne/USDA Agricultural Research Service/Bugwood.org: 48t. David Pearson/Alamy: 36t. Alexander Potapov/Shutterstock: 14cb. prill/istockphoto: 24bc. Rezkerr/Dreamstime: 46tl. Rob Routledge/ Sault College/Bugwood.org: 40obr, 54ctl. Ruestz/CC Wikimedia Commons. Some rights reserved: 42br. Salva/istockphoto: 9cr. s-a-m/ istockphoto: 40tr. http://www.santabarbarachocolate.com: 46br, 51br. Satori13/istockphoto: 18b. 7000/istockphoto: 40c. Silvanbachmann/ Dreamstime: 29bl. Simplyphotos/istockphoto: 17tl. Danny Smythe/Dreamstime: 29br. Snowmanradio/CC Wikimedia Commons. Some rights reserved: 29cl. spet/istockphoto: 54cr. Squirrel77/Dreamstime: 29tr. starceasilviu/istockphoto: 28br. State Library of Queensland: 12bl. SuperStock: 59b. Szefei/istockphoto: 14crba. tristan tan/Shutterstock: 46c. Tatyanaego/Dreamstime: 29rca. Taysh/istockphoto: 28cr. thompsonfamily@bigpond.com: 25cl. tilo/istockphoto: 15b. Trufero/istockphoto: 24cr. AlbyDeTweede/istockphoto: 30t. twildlife/istockphoto: 31bl. Jitka Unv/istockphoto: 46bl. Marcos Velga/Alamy: 52t. Luc Viatour/CC Wikimedia Commons. Some rights reserved: 43c. Michael Vigliotti/Shutterstock: 14cb. Evgeny Vorobeiv/Dreamstime: 28cla. CC Wikipedia: 21b. CC Wikipedia: 21b, 27t. Mark Wilson/CC Wikimedia Commons. Some rights reserved: 52b. Martin N Withers/FLPA: 43tl. xpixel/Shutterstock: front cover tr. Lucy Ya/Shutterstock: front cover bc. Leonid Yastremskiy /Dreamstime: 29rcb. Yatigra/istockphoto: 14crbc. Yelena Yemchuk/istockphoto: 34-35. yeowatzup at Flickr/ CC Wikimedia Commons. Some rights reserved: 29cl. Yun Hunage Yong/CC Wikimedia Commons. Some rights reserved: 47br. Zerber/ Shutterstock: 14c. Kenraiz Krystof Ziarnek/CC Wikimedia Commons. Some rights reserved: 38br. Bernd Zoller/Alamy: 49tl. Every attempt has been made to clear copyright. Should there be any inadvertent omission please apply to the publisher for rectification.

I Love This Tree

Anna Claybourne

Illustrated by Andy Elkerton

W
FRANKLIN WATTS
LONDON·SYDNEY

Contents

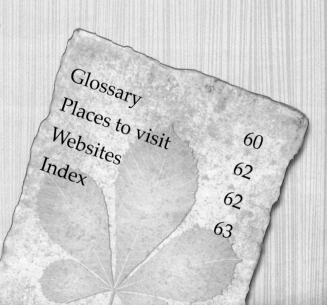

I love this tree

Close to my house, there's a beautiful, huge, spreading sweet chestnut tree. I see it every day. We walk past it on the way to school, and hear the wind rustling through it at night. It's always been there, as long as I can remember.

I love the tree in winter, when its branches are bare, and snow piles up on them, and you can see their beautiful, broad shape.

I love it in spring, when the tree's twigs sprout round, sticky buds, and the tiny fresh new leaves open out.

I love it in summer, when it's hot, and the bright green leaves make dancing, spotted shadows. The leaves seem almost see-through, lit up and glowing in the sunshine.

I love it in autumn, when the tree drops its spiky balls of chestnuts. Then the leaves turn golden brown, break off and flutter down into crunchy piles.

When I think about it, how long has that tree been standing there? Much, much longer than I've been here, that's for sure. It's old and gnarled, and its wide, twisted trunk is covered in green moss.

A young tree

How long ago was the tree young? Maybe hundreds of years ago! What were things like around here in those days? Maybe my home didn't exist, or my school, either. Was there a meadow here, where the tree stands? Or old houses, with people from long ago living in them, wearing old-fashioned clothes and living without cars and electricity? Did they love the tree like I do, and notice it every day?

If the tree wasn't there any more, I would miss it all the time. But it's not just me who would wonder where it had gone! The tree is where squirrels run and hide, and birds nest in spring. Bees buzz around the yellow flowers in summer, and caterpillars eat the leaves. Ants live around the roots, and sometimes, in the dark, we hear owls hooting.

And what if there were no trees at all? It's almost impossible to imagine...

7

A tree in a trillion

This tree is just one of the many, many trees that grow all over our planet.
But just how many trees are there? Millions? Billions? *Trillions*?

The truth is, no one can be sure. There are so many trees, it's impossible to count them all! They grow in gardens and along tree-lined streets, just like my tree. They grow in cool, leafy parks and shady woodlands. They grow in their millions in the mighty conifer forests of the far north, and the hot, damp, tropical rainforests around the equator, stretching as far as the eye can see.

The planet's land areas look mostly green from space, because of all the trees and other plants growing all over it.

The great conifer forests of Russia

Equator

The rainforests of southern Asia

Tropical rainforests

There are even trees growing on high mountains, like the dwarf willow, and in dry, dusty deserts, like the bristlecone pine. Mangrove trees grow at the seashore, their roots at home in the salty waves. Sometimes you even see a tree growing right out of an old, ruined building.

A world of trees

Trees make an enormous difference to our world. They give us all kinds of useful things, from wood and paper to fruit, nuts and flowers. They provide shelter, shade and protection for us, and for countless other creatures too. Did you know trees even help us to breathe?

Bristlecone pine

Mangrove

The Amazon rainforest

Tree counting

🍁 Using satellite images of the Earth's surface, we've worked out that forests cover about one quarter - 25% - of the world's total land area.

🍁 There are probably somewhere around 400 billion, or 400,000,000,000 trees alive at any one time - but this is just a guess, as they cannot all be counted.

🍁 That would mean there are at least 50 trees for every person living on our planet!

🍁 Scientists have counted around 100,000 different species of tree.

What is a tree?

A tree is a plant – a very *big* plant.

Imagine you had never seen a tree – just smaller plants like daisies, tomato plants or sunflowers. Then, one day, you came across a tree for the first time – a big, fully grown tree, like my tall, beautiful chestnut.

You would be AMAZED at how huge a plant could grow! Bigger than you, bigger than a truck, bigger than a whole house! You would stare in amazement at how tall and strong it was, with its massive solid trunk, and great branches reaching up into the sky, waving in the wind. Because we're surrounded by trees all the time, we don't really think about how BIG they are. But trees are the giants of the plant kingdom. In fact, they are giants among all living things.

95 metres

High and mighty

The biggest trees of all, including the coast redwood and the giant sequoia, are truly vast. They are bigger than any type of animal that has ever lived - much bigger than elephants, blue whales, or the biggest dinosaurs. The giant sequoia can grow to 95 metres high - as tall as a 30-floor tower block. A giant sequoia's trunk can reach nearly 9 metres across - so wide, a house could fit inside.

Plants need sunlight to survive. Trees are big, tall and wide because this is a great way for their leaves to reach the sunlight. Growing a wide, strong trunk lets trees grow even taller without falling over. That is why trees are the way they are.

Like other plants, trees stay in one place. They collect what they need from their surroundings: sunlight from the sky, gases from the air, and water from the soil. Trees don't need to walk, swim or fly around to find their food.

Take a closer look

Take a look at this tree, and you'll see all a tree's important parts...

On the branches are the twigs and leaves, flowers or cones, and fruits, nuts or seeds.

A stem (the tree's trunk) carries water and nutrients up from the ground.

Branches grow out from the stem.

Roots grow down into the soil.

11

What a tree sees

Some trees alive today have lived through...

The invention of the wheel
(5,500 years ago)

The building of Egypt's pyramids
(4,600 years ago)

The golden age of ancient Greece
(2,400 years ago)

The invention of gunpowder
(1,000 years ago)

The invention of the printing press
(970 years ago)

Europe's discovery of the Americas
(500 years ago)

Trees can live for a long, long time. We humans come and go, generation after generation, as a big tree grows. Some trees live for hundreds, or even thousands of years.

What about my old chestnut tree? It could be 300 years old or more. So much has changed, since it first sprouted and grew from its seed. Three hundred years ago...

- There were no electric lights – and no cars, trains or aeroplanes.
- There were no computers, phones or televisions.
- Houses didn't have flushing toilets or taps with running water.

During its lifetime, my tree has seen...

1810

... the invention of canned food, in around 1810. Since canning was invented, chestnuts can be used to make tinned chestnut puree.

1890s

... the first motor cars driving by, in the 1890s.

... the first electric streetlights lighting up around it, in the 1890s.

An engraving of the Queen Elizabeth Oak with some visitors, made in 1846, when it was already hundreds of years old.

Trees of history

Some trees have played an important role in history - and some even have their own names.

- Legend tells that Queen Elizabeth I of England was told she had become queen under the Queen Elizabeth Oak. It still stands at Hatfield House, Hertfordshire, England.

- The USA's first president George Washington planted a poplar tree in his garden at Mount Vernon, Virginia in 1785. You can still visit the Washington Tulip Poplar today.

- In Bodh Gaya, India stands the Bodhi Tree, a sacred fig tree planted more than 2,300 years ago. It is said to be related to the tree under which Buddha, the founder of the Buddhist religion, sat.

1900s

... the first airships and planes flying overhead in the 1900s.

1969

... the first trips to the moon in the 1960s and 70s.

1914, 1939

... two world wars, starting in 1914 and 1939.

Birth of a tree

Where did this tree come from?

Like other plants, my chestnut tree grew from a seed – a shiny, brown chestnut. Plants make seeds to create new plants, so that their species survives, even after they die.

What a seed needs

A seed holds food to help it start growing, and instructions to make it grow into the same type of tree as the tree it came from. But it will only start to grow when the conditions are just right.

Long-lasting seeds

• In 2005, a date palm tree grew from a 2,000-year-old seed found in an ancient palace in Israel.

• In 1971, astronauts took sycamore and pine tree seeds on a mission to the moon, then brought them home to be planted around the USA. They are now known as the Moon Trees.

Trees and their seeds

Tree seeds come in many shapes and sizes. They don't always match the size or shape of the tree.

Sweet chestnut tree		Sweet chestnut	
Apple tree		Apple pips	
Sycamore tree		Sycamore seeds	
Coconut palm		Coconut	
Coast redwood - the tallest tree		Coast redwood seeds	

14

Story of a seed

This tree began with a seed that grew on its parent tree. The seed fell down, and fell out of its prickly casing. Somehow, it found its way to this spot.

Maybe it just rolled here.

Maybe a squirrel took the chestnut and hid it here, then never came back.

Maybe someone like me played with the seed, then dropped it.

When it was warm enough, and damp enough, the seed began to grow.

A root grew down into the soil, and a shoot grew up towards the sky.

The shoot began to grow leaves and became a seedling – a baby tree.

It grew stronger, with small branches, and became a sapling – a young tree.

Not all saplings survive. A young tree faces many dangers. It could have been chewed and destroyed by deer or rabbits. It could have been blown down by a storm. People might have cut it down to make way for a field or a house. But this was one of the trees that made it.

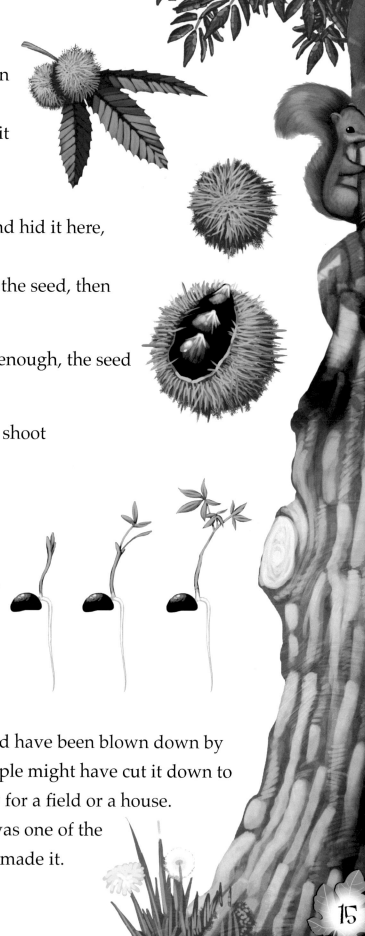

15

Growing bigger

Some plants can grow from a seed, bloom into flower and make their own seeds, all within a year. If you plant a poppy seed, for example, you'll see this happen. But trees are different. They are more like people, who spend a long time being babies, then children, then teenagers, before becoming adults.

Banyan trees in Asia grow extra trunks from roots! They spread out wide, and new roots grow down from the branches to the ground, to help hold them up.

How a tree grows

The sweet chestnut takes between 10 and 30 years to become fully-grown.

By three years old, a chestnut sapling stands around 1 metre tall.

The trunk grows thicker, building strong wood inside, and thick, protective bark outside.

By 10 years old, the tree has spread out into a wider shape, with lots of branches.

A sweet chestnut's full height is around 30 metres. The thicker and stronger the trunk grows, the more branches it can support.

As a tree gets older, its trunk keeps growing wider, but its branches slow down and stop growing.

3 years

10 years

30 years

At home in the branches

Around the world, many animals make their homes, rest, shelter or look for food among tree branches.

• Birds, *bees* and orangutans make their nests in trees.

• Koalas and *sloths* spend most of their lives up a tree.

• Leopards sleep on tree branches, and drag their prey up there to keep it safe.

• Chimpanzees and monkeys sit high up in the trees to pick and eat tasty fruit.

• Snakes, *lizards*, beetles and bugs find places in the branches to hide, or sneak up on prey.

Bendy branches

Branches are bendy and springy so that trees can move with the wind or bend under heavy snow - but if they are pulled or pushed too far, they will break.

Slowcoach ... Olive trees grow ve-r-r-ry slowly. They can take 50 years to grow 5 metres high.

Speedy! The Leyland cyprus tree grows super-fast and can reach 10 metres in 10 years. People use it to make quick, thick hedges.

Tree rings

If you look inside the trunk of a tree that's been cut down, you'll see the beautiful, circular growth rings. Each year, as a tree grows, new rings appear. The number of tree rings in a tree's trunk can reveal the tree's age. I wonder how many rings my chestnut holds?

What makes the rings?

Tree rings are made up of layers of lighter and darker wood. Some people think the rings show the summers and winters the tree has lived through, but that's not quite right. Trees don't grow at all in winter!

The paler section of a tree ring is called springwood or earlywood. It grew in the spring. This is light wood that grew quickly. It carried water up to the tree's branches and leaves.

The darker section is called the summerwood or latewood. It grew in late summer each year, when growing slowed down. As this wood is thicker and harder, it helped to hold the tree up.

Big trunk

Baobab trees store water in their trunk, which grows incredibly wide. Because of this, the wood is soft and spongy, and the growth rings can fade away to nothing.

Clues in the rings

Written in the rings of the old chestnut tree is a record of all the years that have gone by, and some of the things that happened.

• In years when there wasn't much rainfall, the tree grew more slowly - making narrower rings. A wide ring means the tree had a good year for growing. If the tree survived a fire, it shows up as a dark fire-scar.

• The old chestnut tree probably lived through 1816, the 'year without a summer'. In 1815, the mighty volcano Mount Tambora erupted in Indonesia. Ash and dust blocked out sunlight for a whole year, making it hard for plants to grow. This shows up in tree rings too. Many of them are missing a ring for 1816.

First-year growth

Rainy period

Dry period

Scar from forest fire

Mount Tambora erupts

Ring spotting

You can still see the rings in objects that have been made from wood. Look at tables, cupboards or wooden doors in your house to see if you can spot them.

Reaching down

When I look at my old chestnut tree, I know there's another whole part of it that I can't see. A tree has roots that reach deep and spread wide into the soil.

Mirror image?

You may have heard that a tree's roots look like an upside-down version of the tree. This isn't really true. Tree roots don't reach down as deep as the tree is high. Instead, they spread out as wide as they can, but stay quite close to the surface of the ground.

Why? In many places, soil is not that deep. There's usually a layer of hard bedrock underneath it. Also, tree roots need to reach oxygen and water. Soil close to the surface has more oxygen, and gets soaked with water when it rains.

Some roots stick out a bit above the ground. Sometimes you trip over them!

Lateral (side) roots

Absorbing roots reach close to the surface to catch rain.

Heart roots

Sinker roots reach down the deepest.

Growing in the dark

Trees use sunlight to grow, soaking it up in their leaves. But roots can't do that. It's too dark! Instead, roots take food from the rest of the tree, and use this to grow.

How do roots know to grow down?

The tree doesn't have a brain, but it KNOWS which way is down. Roots contain special cells called statocytes that have tiny grains inside them. Gravity pulls the grains downward, and this tells the roots which way to grow.

Sucking up water

Like all living things, trees need water to stay alive. The roots take in water, and nutrients from the soil, and send them to the rest of the tree.

The roots need to reach and soak up as much water as possible. They usually have tiny hairs to help them do this. Many trees also have a type of fungus growing on their roots. It has more hair-like parts that soak up extra water for the tree. In return, the fungus takes food from the tree for itself.

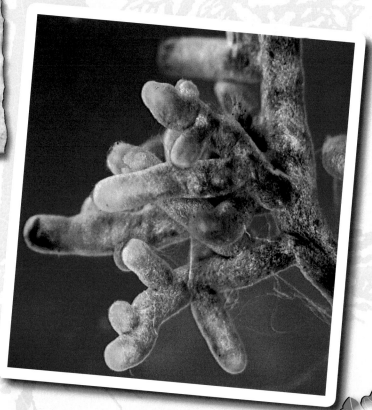

This picture taken by a microscope shows a tree's root hairs and the tiny fungus hairs attached to it.

21

Holding fast

The chestnut tree couldn't stay standing without its great roots. It would soon tip or blow over.

The roots grow into the soil, getting bigger, thicker and stronger as the tree grows higher. They grasp the soil and weigh the tree down, holding it firm, even when the wind blows hard.

The larger roots are made of solid wood, like a tree's trunk. The smaller roots reach out into the soil, making a 'mat' that anchors the tree into the soil firmly.

Uprooted!

This is why it's incredibly hard to uproot a tree. My great chestnut tree has stood firm through 300 years of thunderstorms, windstorms and heavy snow. Sometimes, winds are SO strong that they can blow trees down – even big ones. When this happens, a tree may snap and break off near the base of the trunk. Or it may fall over, pulling up some of its roots, while others break off. But however terrible the storm, you'll never see a tree's whole root system pulled out of the ground in one piece. It holds on way too tight!

Super roots!

Roots have to push hard as they grow, to force their way through thick, heavy soil. In towns and cities, you'll sometimes see roots that have pushed their way through pavements or walls – or whatever gets in their way!

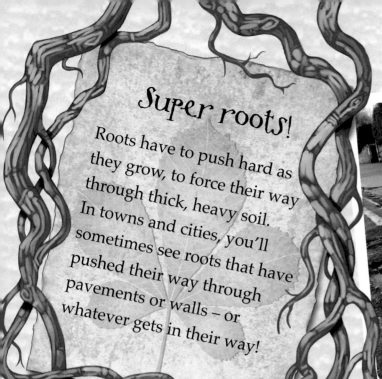

Soil savers

Trees need soil, of course. But did you know that soil also needs trees? In wet, windy places and on hillsides, soil only stays where it is because of trees and their roots. They act as a framework, holding the soil in place.

Farmers have often found that if they clear away all the trees to make space for crops, the soil doesn't last long. It gets blown away by the wind and washed away by rain. With the trees there, though, other plants can grow, in the spaces between the tree trunks. So trees give other plants a place to live, as well as animals.

Root-dwellers

While some creatures make their homes in a tree's branches, others are living in and around the roots, in the darkness beneath my feet.

Living soil

Soil is packed with living things. There are lots of tiny, invisible bacteria living there. So many that, if you held your two hands together and filled them with soil, you would be holding billions and billions of bacteria – more of them, in fact, than there are human beings on the whole of planet Earth.

Who lives here?

Mushrooms grow around tree trunks and roots.

Worms burrow through the soil, swallowing it and taking food from it as they go.

Insects such as ants and bumble bees make nests or burrows in the soil around tree roots. They lay their eggs there, or shelter in the burrow for the winter.

Truffles are fungi that grow underground among some types of tree root. They taste delicious and are very expensive!

Large animals like foxes, badgers and rabbits often live in burrows under trees. The roots hold the soil together, so the burrow is less likely to collapse.

Some insects lay their eggs on tree roots so that their larvae (babies) can feed on the roots when they hatch. This fat baby bug is a witchetty grub, a type of moth larvae from Australia.

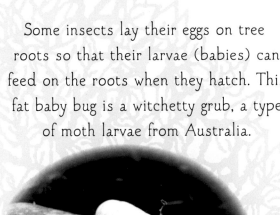

Winter food store

Squirrels store food for the winter, and so do trees! The roots have a store of food, so that when spring comes, the tree can use this to start growing new buds and leaves as quickly as possible.

Out of my space!

Tree roots don't just grow big enough to support and supply their own tree. Scientists have found they actually spread out further than they need to, in order to stop other trees from growing too close. They are like guards, keeping an area around the tree clear and safe from invaders.

Useful roots

Roots can even be useful for us. They can be carved like wood to make tools, sculptures or furniture. Some people use coconut palm roots as a dye or a medicine, or to make natural toothbrushes like these!

Built from wood

What makes a tree a tree, and not any other kind of plant?
Besides its size, the answer is WOOD.

A tree is so big, and reaches out so far, the trunk and the branches have to be really, really strong. Yet they must bend in the wind, and survive all weathers. Only wood can do this job.

Wonderful wood

As my chestnut tree grew, it built up layers and layers of tough wood to give it the strength it needs.

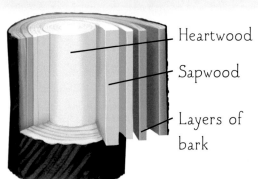

Heartwood

Sapwood

Layers of bark

Brilliant bark

Bark is a tree's skin. Like our own skin, it's made up of layers, and keeps out water and germs. If they get in, the wood inside can start to rot away.

The hard wood in the middle of the trunk, called heartwood, is actually dead, like your hair. Around the edge is the still growing, living wood, or sapwood.

Wood can bend and spring back without breaking. That means it's very hard to snap a tree trunk.

Of course, a tree trunk is big and heavy – but wood is actually quite a lightweight material. It has to be, so the tree doesn't collapse under its own weight.

Made to measure

As a tree's woody trunk and branches grow, they feel their way and sense their surroundings. They will change direction to grow around an obstacle. Sometimes a tree's trunk will even slowly

surround a street sign, fence, bench or abandoned vehicle, and seem to swallow it up.

A tree on its own in a windy place, or at the edge of a forest, grows shorter and thicker than normal, so it's better at resisting the wind. This makes the edge of a forest look gently rounded.

Some trees make themselves extra-strong and bendy by growing a spiral-shaped, twisted trunk, like my chestnut tree.

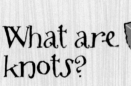

What are knots?

The circles or knots you see in wood form where a branch grows out from the trunk.

Live or green knot

Dead or loose knot

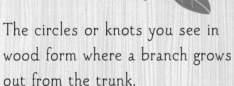

Useful wood

Imagine life without wood! Think of all the things around you that would suddenly disappear, if wood didn't exist.

Tables and chairs, cupboards and doors...

Floorboards, shelves and skirting boards...

Whole wooden houses, log cabins and sheds...

Hollow trees

Because the heartwood in the middle of a tree is dead, it can sometimes rot away or even be burned in a fire, leaving a tree that is hollow, but still alive and growing. Hollow trees provide living spaces for animals like bees and owls. Sometimes the hollow is so big, people can fit inside.

... and all the paper and card we use (and all the books, letters and boxes that are made from it).

Rayon and viscose fabric are made from wood too.

Pencils, lolly sticks, matches, toys, wooden spoons – what other wooden things can you see around you?

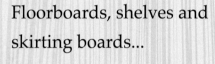

World of wood

Humans have been using wood for thousands of years – probably millions. As well as being good for burning, it's also easy to cut and carve, flexible, strong, feels warm and smooth, and floats.

We use wood a lot today – but it was even more important in the past. Now, we make lots of things from metal and plastic. Long ago, people relied on wood to make machinery, tools, weapons and even shoes. They collected wood to burn for heating and cooking. Bicycles, bathtubs and horse-drawn carriages were made of wood. Floating logs, hollowed out to make a place to sit, were the first boats.

Which wood is which?

Soft, quick-growing pine wood is used to make paper.

Mahogany, rosewood and walnut trees are prized for the beautiful colours of their wood.

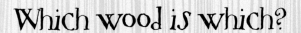

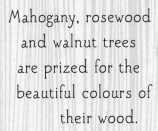

Hard, heavy oak makes the strongest furniture and wooden beams for building.

The world's most valuable Stradivarius violins were made from carefully chosen spruce, willow (left) and maple wood.

Sweet chestnut wood is very weatherproof, so you'll find it in fences and garden furniture.

Woodworking wasps

Making paper from wood was copied from the way wasps chew wood to make their papery nests.

29

Wood and bark creatures

Wood and bark are hard and solid, yet some creatures can still nibble or dig their way inside.

Into the wood

Woodpeckers hammer on trees with their strong beaks to bore holes in them. Do they get a headache? No! Woodpeckers have extra-thick skulls and strong neck muscles to make their job easier. They can make a hole big enough to build a nest in, or a smaller one to hunt for insects that live under the bark.

The female wood wasp drills almost two centimetres deep into the wood of a pine tree to lay her eggs. She also squirts in a fungus to rot the wood. When the larvae hatch, they munch on the rotting wood.

Bark and branch munchers

We may eat fruit and nuts from trees, but for some animals, the bark is a good food. Rabbits love to nibble away at the bark of young trees. Deer often chew bark too, especially in winter when there's not much other food around.

As for elephants, they can kill large numbers of trees as they feed. If it can't reach the branches, an elephant will push a tree over. Then it uses its trunk to tear the branches off, and gobble them up, with the leaves and fruit.

Beaver dams

If you're a riverside tree, the last creature you want to see is a beaver. Besides feeding on twigs, leaves and bark, beavers gnaw right through trees until they topple them over. They use the wood to build big dams across rivers. Inside is the beavers' home, or lodge, with underwater entrances to keep them safe from predators.

fighting back!

Some trees fight back by releasing sticky resin to trap and stop bark-invading insects. Have you ever seen a piece of amber with an insect trapped inside? Amber is fossilised tree resin, from pine trees that lived millions of years ago.

Green and leafy

As you walk under a big chestnut tree in summer, you're shaded by its thousands of soft, spreading, green leaves, gently waving and rustling together. What are all those leaves for?

Sun catchers

Think about what most plants have in common. They're all green! Leaves are the green parts of plants, and they hold the secret to keeping the plant alive.

Plants need light to grow and live – mainly sunlight. To use the light, plants have to collect it and soak it up, and this is the job leaves do. Trees are big, so they need a lot of light. And that means they need a lot of leaves.

Leaves or needles?

The chestnut tree's leaves are flat and wide, to catch all the light they can. They spread out all around the tree, so the sun can shine on each and every leaf.

But not all leaves are flat. Some trees, like conifers, have narrow, pointed leaves instead, called needles. They also soak up sunlight, but are tougher. They don't lose water and dry up as easily as flat leaves do, and they are better at surviving tough winter weather.

Sometimes green, or evergreen?

Like many trees, the sweet chestnut loses all its leaves in the autumn. The leaves turn brown and gold, then fall down, making a crunchy carpet on the ground, but leaving the tree's branches bare. Then, in the spring, new leaves grow. This kind of tree is called a deciduous tree.

But some trees, like most conifers and holly trees, do not drop all their leaves in winter. They keep their tough, dark green leaves or needles all year round. They are the evergreen trees.

Their leaves do fall off – just not all at once. Each leaf or needle grows old, dies and drops off by itself, and a new one replaces it. Trees near the equator, where there is no winter, are also evergreen.

Talking trees

Trees can actually talk to each other using their leaves. If insects attack a willow tree, its leaves release a chemical into the air that other willow trees can detect as a danger warning. When they do, they pump bad-tasting chemicals into their own leaves to put the insects off.

Energy from the sun

What are a tree's leaves for? They are its food factories. They use sunlight to make the food the tree needs.

Inside the leaves, water from the ground and gas from the air are changed into food chemicals. The leaf uses light energy from the sun to make this work. The tree then uses the food to grow and build all its parts: new wood, leaves and branches, flowers and fruits.

The process is called photosynthesis. 'Photo' means light, and 'synthesis' means combining or putting together. So this word really means 'putting things together with light'.

What goes in?

The tree's leaves receive water and useful chemicals from the ground. The roots suck them up, then they travel through tiny tubes called xylem to all the upper parts of the tree.

The leaf takes in sunlight through its surface, which lets light through.

The leaf also needs carbon dioxide, a gas found in the air. It takes this in through tiny holes on the underside of the leaf, called stomata. Stomata are microscopically small. They look like this close up.

34

What happens inside?

Inside the leaves, a green chemical called chlorophyll soaks up the sun's energy. The energy is then used to build food chemicals, using ingredients from the water and carbon dioxide.

What goes out?

After photosynthesis happens, a different gas, oxygen, is left over. It comes out of the leaves through the stomata.

Water escapes through the stomata.

The food chemicals pass out of the leaf through its stalk, and into the rest of the tree.

Shapes of leaves

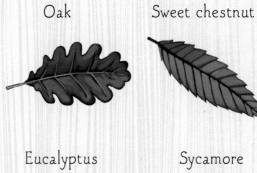

You can recognise different types of tree by their leaf shapes.

Oak   Sweet chestnut

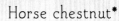

Eucalyptus   Sycamore

Beech   Rowan

Jacaranda   Horse chestnut*

* Not a true chestnut tree. Its nuts look similar, but humans can't eat them.

35

Breathing leaves

Trees breathe! Instead of lungs, they breathe using their leaves. They breathe in the gas they need, carbon dioxide, and breathe out a different gas, oxygen.

This is very lucky for us. In fact, it's essential for us! Humans and other animals need oxygen. We breathe in oxygen, and breathe out carbon dioxide.

Healthy air

This means that all the trees and other plants on the planet are constantly taking away our waste gas, carbon dioxide, and replacing it with the oxygen we need. They make the air fresh and healthy for humans and other animals.

If you have plants in your home or classroom, they help to keep the air there healthy.
If you have lots of gardens, parks and trees around where you live, they keep the air fresh too. But this also works on a much bigger scale – for the whole of our planet, the Earth.

The planet's lungs

The Earth is surrounded by a layer of air, called the atmosphere, made up of a mixture of gases.

As trees and other plants breathe, they help to keep the amount of carbon dioxide gas in the air at a healthy, safe level. The atmosphere is constantly swirling around and being mixed up, so you don't have to be close to trees or plants for this to help you. The Earth's huge forests and jungles, spread over several large areas, constantly help to balance the mixture of gases in the air. So do the millions of other plants on land, and the plant plankton (tiny floating plants) in the sea.

What's in the air?

28% nitrogen

1% carbon dioxide, argon, water vapour and other gases

21% oxygen

Too hot!

Burning fuel - like the petrol in a car, or the coal in a power station - releases carbon dioxide too. Because of cars, planes, factories and power stations, we now release more carbon dioxide than we used to.

Scientists think that extra carbon dioxide in the air acts like a blanket, holding in heat and making our planet warm up. This is known as global warming. If it gets too warm, it could affect our weather and wildlife, melt ice and make sea levels rise. So we need trees and other plants more than ever, to help keep the carbon dioxide in the atmosphere balanced.

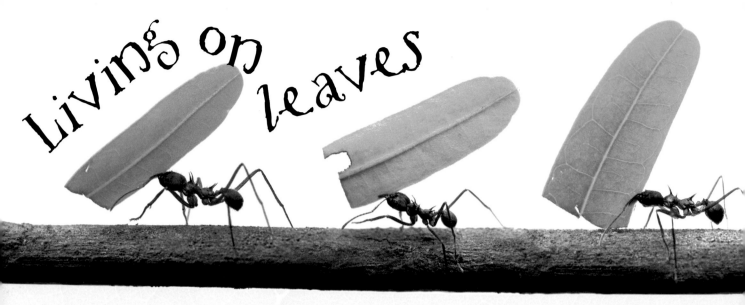

Living on leaves

Crawling above are some leafcutter ants, carrying sections of tree leaves. The adult ants drink the leaves' sap, or juice. They also use the leaves to grow a type of fungus, which is fed to their babies.

Leaf-lovers

Delicious, fresh, green, juicy tree leaves are an important food for all kinds of animal – from tiny beetles to the tallest of all, the giraffe. Giraffes evolved to have long necks because a long neck gives them a survival advantage. It lets them reach high into trees to collect more young-juicy leaves.

A few animals stick to just one type of tree – like the koala, which prefers only eucalyptus leaves. Forest tent caterpillars eat so much, they can destroy trees and even forests. They hatch from eggs laid by moths on oak, aspen and maple trees. Then they march all over the tree, munching the branches bare.

Inside out

The leaf miner moth caterpillar lives inside a leaf, nibbling away between its upper and lower surface.

38

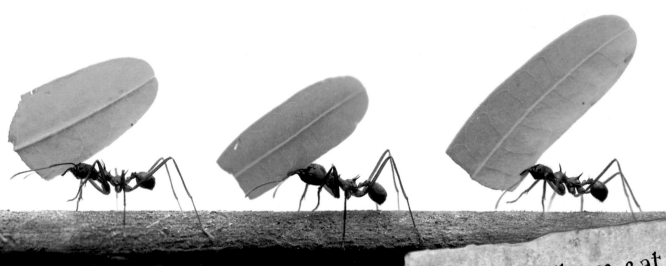

Leafy nests

Leaves make a soft, comfy nest. Chimps use a fresh pile of leaves to make themselves a new nest every night.

Weaver ants work in teams to make nests from leaves. They pull leaves together, then fix them in place using sticky silk made by the ant larvae (babies). One tree can contain dozens of leaf nests.

Tailor birds 'sew' leaves to make their nests. They make holes in the leaves, then thread plant fibres through to stitch them together.

Leaf tools

Orangutans use leaves as napkins to wipe their faces, or as gloves to protect their hands when picking spiny fruits, or as a makeshift umbrella.

Why don't we eat tree leaves?

Humans eat lettuce and cabbage leaves, but most tree leaves are too tough or bitter-tasting for us. We use a few types of tree leafs, like bay leaves and kaffir lime leaves, as seasoning.

Bursting into flower

In summer, after growing its leaves all spring, the chestnut tree bursts into bloom. Its flowers grow in feathery, finger-shaped creamy-white and

pink clusters. This type of flower is called a catkin, as it's a bit like a cat's tail. The flowers are also called the tree's 'candles'.

The huge chestnut covered with flowers is a beautiful sight, but the flowers have a very strong smell. Some people like it, while it makes others feel ill. It's been described as smelling like honey, overripe fruit or even fried mushrooms!

What are flowers for?

Chestnut trees belong to the biggest plant family, the flowering plants. Flowers (and pine cones) have an important job to do. They make the plant's seeds, which can then grow into new plants.

Not all plants, or all trees, have flowers.

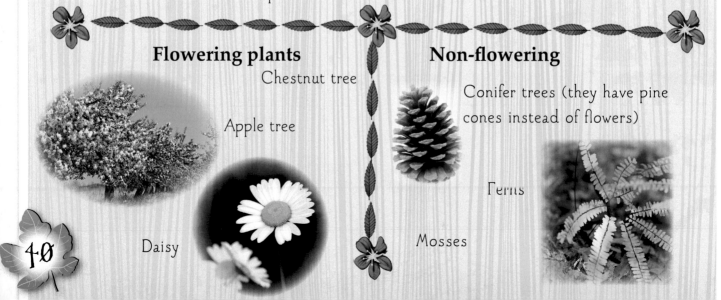

Flowering plants

Chestnut tree

Apple tree

Daisy

Non-flowering

Conifer trees (they have pine cones instead of flowers)

Ferns

Mosses

Making seeds

Most trees make two types of flower: male and female! Sometimes, they grow on separate male and female trees, like this holly tree. But the sweet chestnut tree contains both male and female flowers.

Male flowers release powdery yellow pollen. To make seeds, the pollen has to land on the female flowers – a process called pollination. Pollination makes the female flower grow a fruit, pod or case, with the seeds inside.

Pollen carriers

How does pollen get from the male flower to the female flower? It can blow there in the wind. But there is another way too. Flowers contain a sugary food called nectar. Insects come to feed on it, and pollinate the plant at the same time, as they fly from one flower to the next. Flowers have strong smells and bright colours to help insects find them.

Aaaaachooo!

Pollen in the wind is what gives some people hayfever, making them sneeze.

flower power

In their quest to attract bees and other insects, tree flowers have developed an amazing range of beautiful shapes, colours and scents.

The magnolia has stunning large cream, pink or purple flowers.

Lilac flowers grow in thick clusters. Their gorgeous, sweet scent hangs in the air.

The ylang-ylang tree's star-shaped flowers have a unique and lovely smell. They are used to make perfume.

Australia's eucalyptus tree flowers look like something from a sci-fi movie!

Banana trees grow some of the biggest and most striking flowers of all.

flower food

The nectar trees make in their flowers feeds many animals – mainly insects and birds, as they can fly up to reach the high branches.

A hummingbird flaps its wings up to 80 times a second to hover completely still in mid-air, while its long tongue reaches into a flower for nectar.

Honey possums are tiny tree mammals with long, snouts and tongues for eating nectar.

flower flavours

We use some tree flowers as food too – especially elderflowers, which are used to make drinks. The flowers of the prickly sesban tree are a popular vegetable in parts of Asia.

Some insects and spiders camouflage themselves to look exactly like flowers, to help them hide from enemies or sneak up on prey.

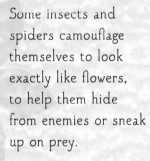

flower festival

Every spring in Japan, everyone celebrates the blooming of the cherry tree blossom with a festival. The pink blossoms cover the trees, then flutter down and carpet the ground. People have picnics under the trees to enjoy the blossom.

Back to the beginning

My tree has grown for hundreds of years, starting as a tiny seedling. It grew bigger and stronger, sprouted leaves and branches, and finally flowers and fruits. But one day, the chestnut tree will die. It cannot live forever – but it can make more sweet chestnuts, so that its species stays alive. That is why trees make seeds.

How seeds form

Once a female flower has been pollinated, it can make seeds. In a sweet chestnut, the female flowers are at the bottom of the catkins, so that is where the seeds grow.

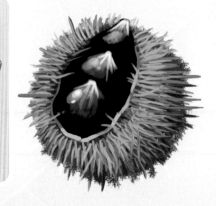

The flower petals dry up and start to fall off. The base of the flower swells up. The fruit, shell or pod around the seeds usually forms from all or part of the flower. In a sweet chestnut, this is a thick, green, spiky case. Inside, the seeds grow and ripen, until they are ready.

What are the spikes for?

The spiny case keeps chestnuts safe from animals while they ripen. Then, the case splits open.

44

A place to grow

The seeds are on the tree – but, of course, they can't grow there. So, as they ripen, they fall onto the ground. If an old tree is dying, one of its seeds might grow into a new tree where it once stood. But not all seeds can do that. During a tree's lifetime, the seeds must find their own spaces to grow in. Trees have clever ways of spreading their seeds far and wide – known as seed dispersal.

Nuts on the move

Chestnuts are big, heavy seeds, so when they fall, they fall close to the tree. They are moved by animals that collect seeds and take them somewhere else to eat or store. Squirrels do this, and so do jays, a type of bird. (And so do humans!)

A ripe chestnut might be dropped on the way, or stashed in a food store, forgotten about, and left to grow.

Other seeds have their own ways of dispersing...

A sycamore seed has a wing-shaped case to help it 'fly' sideways as it falls.

Coconut palms grow by the sea. The coconuts float, so they can travel from one seashore to another on the waves.

Inside fruits and seeds

A chestnut seed looks like a shiny brown flattened ball, with a pointy tip. It's only about 2.5 cm across, but inside it contains all the instructions it needs to grow into a chestnut tree. It's also packed with food, to support the baby plant until it grows its own leaves and can collect energy from the sun.

Look inside

Seed coat

Food supply

Embryo

The chestnut is covered with a tough skin or seed coat. Inside, it's mostly filled with the nutty, floury food supply. There's also the embryo – a tiny mini-plant, waiting to start growing.

Fruits and seeds

As they grow, chestnuts are surrounded by their spiny cases. Other trees have different versions of this. On a cocoa tree, it's the big cocoa pod (right), containing dozens of cocoa seeds or beans (which we use to make chocolate).

On apple, pear, plum and many other trees, the seeds form inside a soft, juicy fruit. The fruit protects the seeds. But it also helps to disperse the seeds, by tempting animals to eat it. They then spread the seeds, by throwing them away if they don't want to eat them. Or the seeds might pass through their bodies and get spread around in their droppings.

Trees and their fruits

Fruits can have one big seed inside, or many smaller ones.

Apple tree

Apple

Cocoa tree

Cocoa pod and beans

Olive tree

Olives

Carambola

Star fruit

Avocado tree

Avocado

Durian tree

Durian

Ripe fruits, like this orange, often have bright colours to make them easy to spot, and a smell or taste that animals find delicious.

Stinky and spiky

The durian is a big, heavy, spiky fruit that grows in southeast Asia. It tastes nice, but is famous for its revolting stink. It's said to smell like a mixture of onions, toilets and smelly socks! It's so horrible that in some places, it's against the law to take a durian on public transport.

fruit and seed eaters

Chestnut trees, and other trees, make far more fruits and seeds than they need. This is because so many of them will be eaten by animals. Orangutans and monkeys, fruit bats, parrots, butterflies, bugs and lizards are among the animals that feed on trees' fruits and nuts. A type of fish, the pacu of South America, eats nuts that fall from trees into rivers, and even tigers have been seen eating the fruits of the slow match tree.

Vervet monkey in a fig-mulberry tree

Chestnut eaters

Sweet chestnuts alone feed all kinds of different creatures, from tiny insects that burrow inside the nuts, to big, hungry mammals like grizzly bears.

A female chestnut weevil chooses nice firm chestnuts that are just starting to ripen. She makes small holes in them, and lays her eggs inside. The larvae hatch out and nibble away inside the nut. Then, when it drops to the ground, they wriggle out – leaving an empty shell containing only leftovers and weevil poo (top)!

Tree mammals like chipmunks, squirrels and dormice also love chestnuts. The ancient Romans used to feed dormice on a diet of chestnuts to fatten them up before eating them.

Sika deer eating a chestnut

Squirrels are very clever animals. In tests set up by scientists, they have found their way through complicated obstacle courses to get to a precious reward of nuts. Squirrels will also sit in a tree and throw nuts or shells at people or animals to scare them away. Even smarter, they sometimes dig fake hiding holes when other animals are watching, to trick them about where they are really going to hide their nuts.

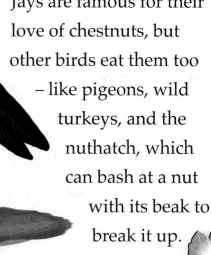
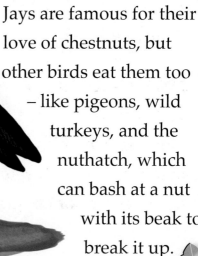

When chestnuts fall to the ground, bigger animals eat them too.

Deer and wild boar will snuffle around through the fallen leaves to find them.

Nuts play an important part in feeding up animals like bears in the autumn, before they hibernate for the winter.

Jays are famous for their love of chestnuts, but other birds eat them too – like pigeons, wild turkeys, and the nuthatch, which can bash at a nut with its beak to break it up.

fruit and seed food

Through history, the sweet chestnut has been a lifesaving tree. My tree could have saved someone from starving!

People have been growing and farming chestnut trees for at least 4,000 years, to use their nuts as food. A chestnut contains almost everything humans need to survive – carbohydrates (which give you energy), protein, fat, fibre and lots of vitamins, especially Vitamin C. In the past, when crops failed, people and farm animals could survive eating hardly anything but sweet chestnuts.

Cooking chestnuts

You can roast, fry or boil chestnuts, or even eat them raw. Long ago, people dried them and ground them up into flour to make bread or cakes. The chestnut tree was sometimes called the 'bread tree'.

Today, chestnuts are more of a luxury food. Chestnut sweets, puddings and cakes are served at Christmas in France, and at New Year in Japan. In a lot of places, they are a street snack, cooked on a mobile chestnut-roasting cart.

Horse chestnuts

Don't get sweet chestnuts mixed up with horse chestnuts, or conkers. They are not edible!

Tree farms

We grow and harvest many other tree fruits and seeds too. A field or farm of trees being grown for crops is sometimes called an orchard. Some countries depend on their fruit harvests to make money.

Instant Mont Blanc

Try sweet chestnuts yourself by making this easy version of Mont Blanc pudding, named after a snow-capped mountain on the border between Italy and France.

You will need:
Ready-made mini meringue nests
A tin of ready-to-eat sweetened chestnut purée
Instant whipped cream

Spoon a small, mountain-shaped pile of chestnut puree on top of each meringue. Use the cream to add a snowy peak on top, along with a cherry or chocolate sprinkles if you like.

Billions of apples, oranges and bananas are grown every year, to eat, cook or make into juice.

Coffee and cocoa trees give us two of the world's favourite things: coffee and chocolate.

Huge areas of farmland are used for oil palm trees. They make oil used in cooking, processed foods, soap and washing powder, and even biofuel for running cars.

51

The end

Like all living things, one day this tree will stop living. There will be a time when it no longer stands here. Its shade, its rustling leaves, its wide, strong branches, will all be gone. What will happen to it in the end?

Why do trees die?

As a tree gets very old, its bark, branches and twigs grow weak. They are more easily damaged by wind, ice and snow. Germs and diseases can get in, and the tree starts to rot and decay. This makes it weaker still, and eventually it dies.

Some very tall trees, like coast redwoods, eventually die because they are too big. It gets harder and harder for them to suck all the water they need right to the top of the tree. They start to weaken and dry out.

The oldest tree

No one can be sure which is the oldest living tree of all. It's thought to be a bristlecone pine tree growing in the White Mountains in California, USA, which is over 5,000 years old.

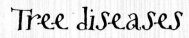

Tree diseases

Some types of fungus and mould invade under tree bark and feed on the wood. Others attack the leaves or needles, covering them with brown blotches, or making them wither and die.

Sweet chestnuts can fall victim to one of the worst diseases of all – chestnut blight, a fungus that invades the bark. Once it grows all the way around the trunk, the tree cannot survive.

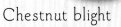

Chestnut blight

falling down

When a tree is dead, it stops growing leaves, and its brittle branches start to snap off. It looks bare, grey and dried out. But a dead tree doesn't usually fall down straight away. My chestnut tree could stand for another 20 or 30 years after it dies. Eventually, though, a dead tree will topple over, or get blown down in a storm. Or, if it's in a city, park or garden, someone might cut it down first, so it can't fall on anyone.

Space to grow

In forests, a tree dying and falling down is part of the natural cycle of growth. It lets in light for other plants, and for new baby trees to start growing.

Life in a log

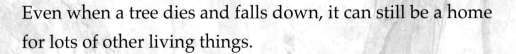

Even when a tree dies and falls down, it can still be a home for lots of other living things.

Log~dwellers

Mosses, lichens and even grass and small plants eventually start to grow on fallen dead trees. They make a home for small animals, like beetles, flies, millipedes and tiny worms.

Animals like lizards and birds will then visit the log to catch insects to eat. A bear, snake, hedgehog or spider might use a hollow fallen tree as a place to hibernate.

Lichen

Brown bear

Millipede

Fox

Weasel

If a fallen tree has a hollow inside, it can make a shelter or home for all kinds of animals, such as foxes, mice, weasels, bats, owls or toads.

Long-eared bat

Dead wood

We can't eat dead wood, but some other creatures can. When fungi settle on an old log, their roots reach down into it and feed on it, slowly breaking it down into crumbly dirt. Termites (below) also nibble away at dead wood. They have tiny micro-organisms living inside them that help them digest the wood and get food from it.

As there can be millions of termites in a colony, they can eat up dead wood very quickly. It then comes out in their droppings and becomes part of the soil. It's thanks to things like fungi and termites that fallen trees eventually crumble away and disappear. Otherwise, there would be millions of them everywhere we went!

Recycled trees

As a tree rots, crumbles or gets nibbled away, all the valuable energy in it gets recycled. It is used by other animals, or falls back into the soil. It may become food for new, younger trees. In this way, the chestnut tree, and every other tree, can go on forever.

People and trees

People have always loved trees. It's not just because they are so useful. Something about trees makes us feel calm, relaxed and peaceful.

A tree is so much bigger than you are, its spreading branches can shelter you from the sun and rain, and make you feel safe. Deciduous trees connect us to the changing seasons.

Being near a tree means being close to nature and wildlife. It means birds, butterflies, bees and beetles, moss and mushrooms, fresh new buds and leaves.

At night, the trees roar, rustle, wave and whisper, reminding us that they are still there, still standing safely over us.

A tree can be a place to hide, to build a treehouse, climb or play. And a whole forest feels like an enchanted world.

56

We have written poems, songs and proverbs since ancient times to express our feelings about the power and beauty of trees...

The best time to plant a tree was 20 years ago. The next best time is now.
Chinese Proverb

Every green tree is far more glorious than if it were made of gold and silver.
Martin Luther King

Friendship is a sheltering tree.
Samuel Taylor Coleridge

Trees are poems that the Earth writes upon the sky.
Kahlil Gibran

The creation of a thousand forests is in one acorn.
Ralph Waldo Emerson

In a forest of a hundred thousand trees, no two leaves are alike.
Paulo Coelho

Every leaf speaks bliss to me, fluttering from the autumn tree...
Emily Brontë

Tree tales

In the folk tales, myths and legends and magical stories of the world, trees hold great power. Artists have also been inspired by their beauty.

The World Tree

Norse (Viking) mythology is built around Yggdrasil, a giant ash tree. No one sees Yggdrasil, but it spreads out over all of the Earth and sky. Its roots, trunk and branches connect nine different worlds, including the worlds of the gods, the giants, the dead, and our everyday human world.

The Sky Tree

The legends of the Iroquois people, of North America, say that long ago, the Sky People lived in the Sky World, high up in the air. In the middle of the Sky World was a great tree. One day, a man dug up the roots of the tree, because his pregnant wife wanted to eat their bark. But this created a hole in the Sky World, and the Sky Woman fell through. Her grandchildren created the Earth as we know it today, and the Sky Woman's head became the moon.

Yggdrasil, the world tree

The Tree of Knowledge

Several religions feature the story of the Tree of Knowledge, which grows in the Garden of Eden. The first humans, Adam and Eve, are forbidden to eat its fruit, but they eat it anyway, disobeying God. The fruit gives them knowledge of good and evil, and they have to leave the perfect garden and go out into the world.

Trees in art

Many of the world's greatest artists have painted trees – the beautiful cherry trees of the famous Japanese artist Katsushika Hokusai (right), Vincent van Gogh's vibrant olive, mulberry and chestnut tree paintings (below), and the works of modern artists like David Hockney.

Trees in books

Trees can be important characters in books too. Enid Blyton wrote children's books about the Magic Faraway Tree - like Yggdrasil, its branches reach into the clouds, and it is so big there are whole houses hollowed out inside its trunk. In the Harry Potter books, the Whomping Willow is a violent tree that can wave its branches around and attack anyone who comes too close.

Glossary

absorbing roots Tree roots just under the ground surface, that soak up rain.

atmosphere Layer of gases around the Earth.

bacteria A type of tiny living thing.

bedrock Layer of hard rock under the soil.

carbon dioxide A gas that animals breathe out and plants take in through their leaves.

catkin Type of long, fluffy flower that resembles a cat's tail.

chlorophyll Green chemical found in plant leaves.

conifer Type of plant or tree that has cones instead of flowers.

deciduous Deciduous trees lose all their leaves in winter.

digest To take in food and break it down into useful chemicals.

earlywood Wood that a tree grows early in the growing season.

ecosystem A habitat and the group of living things found in it.

embryo Part of a seed that grows into a new plant.

equator Imaginary line around the middle of the Earth, between the Poles.

evergreen Evergreen trees have leaves on them all year round.

fungus A type of living thing that includes moulds and mushrooms.

global warming A gradual increase in temperatures on Earth.

growth rings Rings that form from the way a tree grows each summer.

habitat A place or type of surroundings where living things are found.

heart roots Roots growing downwards below the middle of a tree.

heartwood Dead wood in the middle of a tree trunk.

hibernate To spend the winter in a sleep-like state.

larvae The young of some types of insect.

lateral roots Tree roots that grow out sideways under the ground.

latewood Wood that a tree grows late in the growing season.

micro-organisms Tiny living things that are too small to see without a microscope.

nectar Sweet sugary liquid found inside flowers.

needles The thin, dark green leaves of some types of evergreen tree.

nutrients Food chemicals.

oxygen A gas found in the air, which plants give out and animals breathe in.

photosynthesis The way plants use sunlight, carbon dioxide and water to make food.

plankton Small living things that float around in water.

pollen Yellow powder made by male flowers to help make plant seeds.

pollination Moving pollen from male flowers to female flowers so that seeds can form.

sap Watery liquid that moves around inside a tree or other plant.

sapling A young tree.

sapwood The living wood found in the outer layers of a tree's trunk.

seed coat The outer covering of a seed.

seed dispersal The ways plants spread their seeds out far and wide to grow in new places.

seedling A plant that has just started to grow from a seed.

sinker roots Tree roots that grow downwards from lateral roots.

species A particular type of tree, plant, animal or other living thing.

springwood Wood that a tree grows early in the growing season.

statocytes Special cells that help plants to detect gravity.

stem The main supporting stalk of a plant, which in trees is known as a trunk.

stomata Tiny holes in the lower surface of leaves that let gases in and out.

summerwood Wood that a tree grows late in the growing season.

xylem Tissue made up of tubes that liquid travels along inside a plant.

Places to visit

Royal Botanic Gardens, Kew
Kew, Richmond, Surrey, TW9 3AB, UK
www.kew.org

Westonbirt, the National Arboretum
Tetbury, Gloucestershire, GL8 8QS, UK
www.forestry.gov.uk/westonbirt

Eden Project
Bodelva, Cornwall, PL24 2SG, UK
www.edenproject.com

The New York Botanical Garden
2900 Southern Blvd, Bronx, NY10458,
USA
www.nybg.org

Redwood National and State Parks
c/o Crescent City Information Center
1111 Second Street, Crescent City, CA,
USA
www.nps.gov/redw/index.htm

Monteverde Cloud Forest Reserve
Monteverde, Costa Rica
www.monteverdeinfo.com

Websites

Nature Detectives: Tree Activity Pack
Lots of tree-related printable activity
sheets, games and fun ideas.
www.naturedetectives.org.uk/packs/
trees.htm

Biology4Kids: Plants
Useful basic plant facts and science.
www.biology4kids.com/files/plants_
main.html

Kidzone Science: Trees
Tree facts, diagrams, printables,
activities and links.
www.kidzone.ws/plants/trees.htm

Ecokids: What is a Tree?
Facts and ecological information on
trees and forests.
www.ecokids.ca/pub/eco_info/topics/
forests

Note to parents and teachers: Every effort has
been made by the Publishers to ensure that these
websites are suitable for children, that they are of
the highest educational value, and that they contain
no inappropriate or offensive material. However,
because of the nature of the Internet, it is impossible
to guarantee that the contents of these sites will not
be altered. We strongly advise that Internet access is
supervised by a responsible adult.

Index

Index (continued)